PIANO · VOCAL · GUITAR

HIDDEN FIGURES

MUSIC FROM THE MOTION PICTURE SOUNDTRACK

ISBN 978-1-4950-8954-1

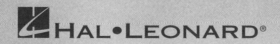

HAL•LEONARD®

7777 W. BLUEMOUND RD. P.O. BOX 13819 MILWAUKEE, WI 53213

In Australia Contact:
Hal Leonard Australia Pty. Ltd.
4 Lentara Court
Cheltenham, Victoria, 3192 Australia
Email: ausadmin@halleonard.com.au

Visit Hal Leonard Online at
www.halleonard.com

KATHERINE

Written by BENJAMIN WALLFISCH,
PHARRELL WILLIAMS and HANS ZIMMER

Moderately, expressively

Pedal ad lib. throughout

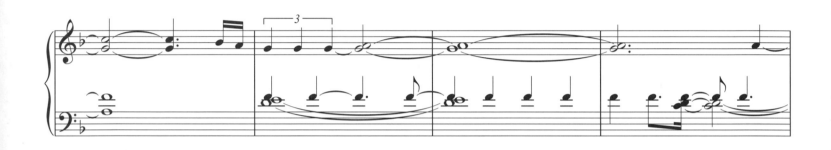

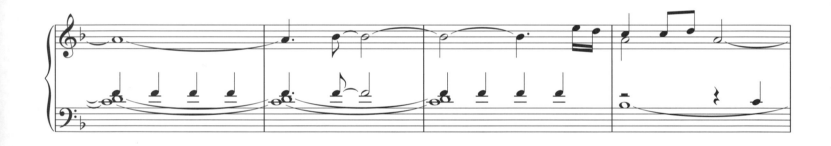

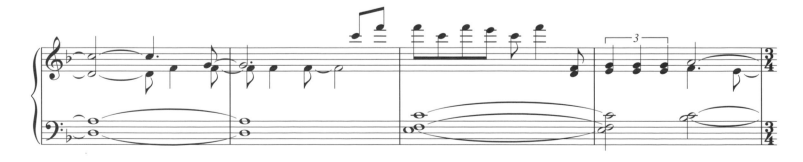

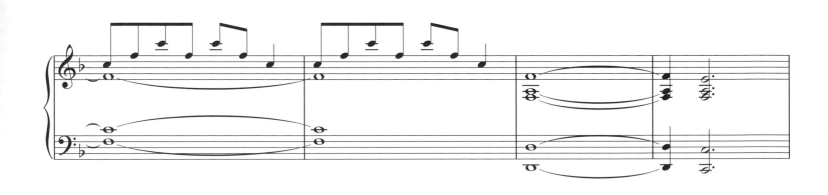

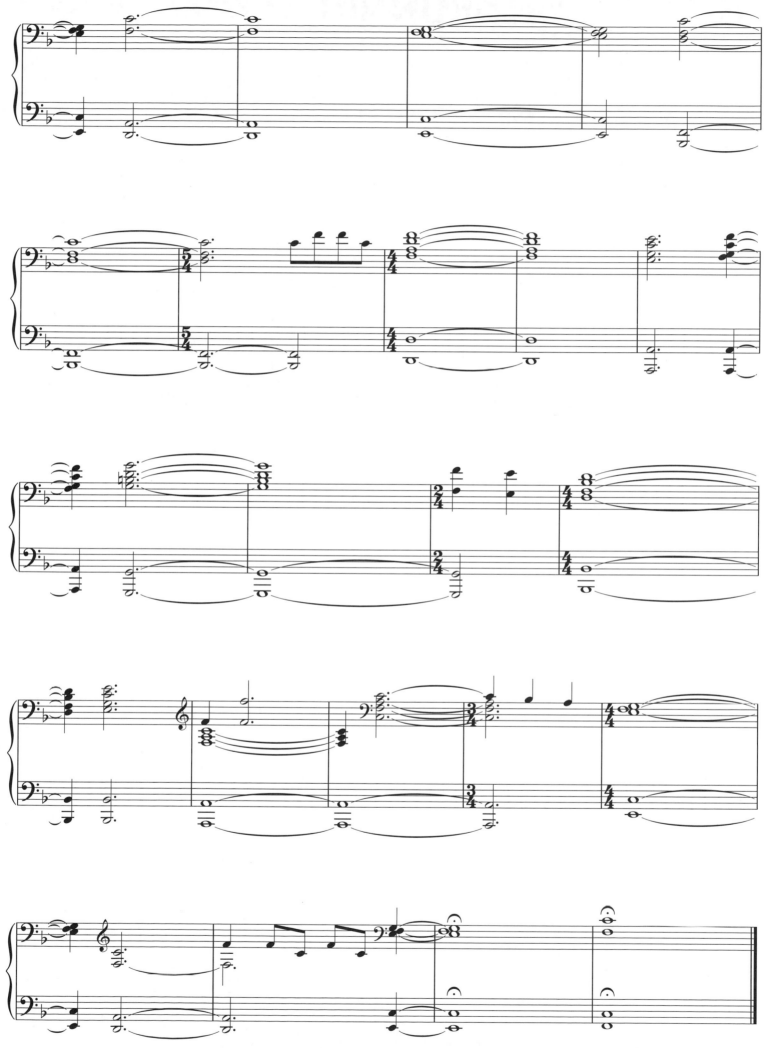

RUNNIN'

Words and Music by
PHARRELL WILLIAMS

Moderately fast

Sum-mer-time _ in Vir-
You and I _ are no

gin-ia _ was an ov-en (ov-en). All the kids _ eat-ing
dif-f'rent _ from each oth-er (oth-er). Shut our eyes _ when we

ice cream _ with their cous-ins (cous-ins). I was stud-y-ing while
slum-ber; _ I see num-bers (num-bers). Black and white _ were com-

CRAVE

Words and Music by
PHARRELL WILLIAMS

SURRENDER

Words and Music by
PHARRELL WILLIAMS

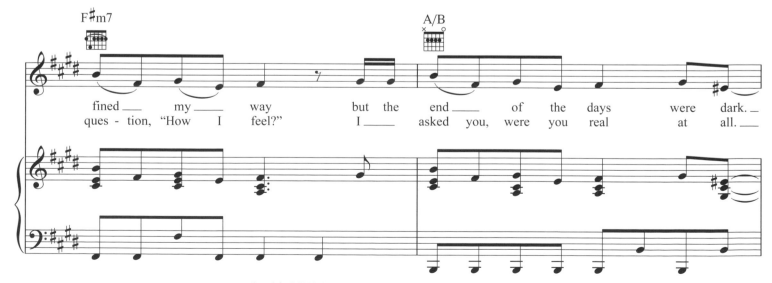

ABLE

Words and Music by
PHARRELL WILLIAMS

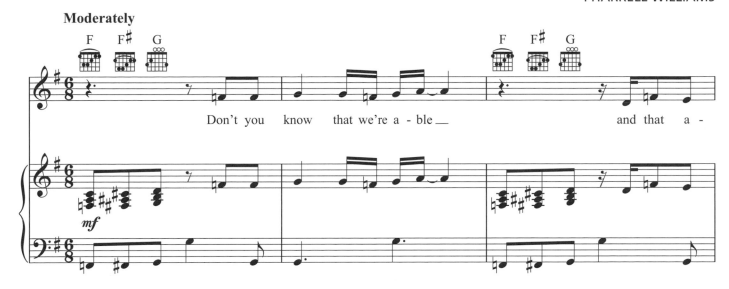

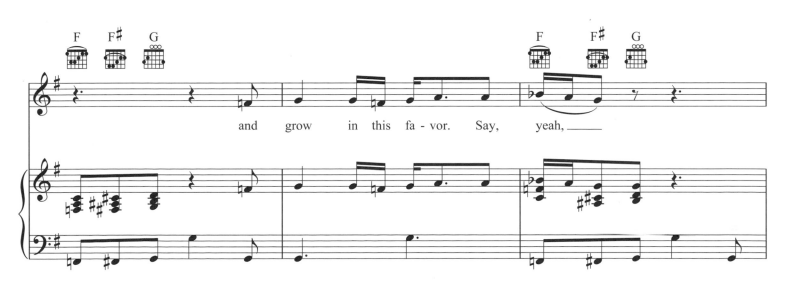

MIRAGE

Words and Music by
PHARRELL WILLIAMS

Try'n' to un-der-stand _ the way I've been be-hav-ing.

It's a fun-ny thing _ you real-ly got _ to see.

Is it just your love _ that's

got me go-ing cra-zy   or my eyes play-ing with me? ___ Hmm. ___

APPLE

Words and Music by PHARRELL WILLIAMS
and ALICIA COOK

Female: Fun-ny thing a-bout the ap-ple, ___ the peach is sweet but ain't the

same, ___ no. The pear com-pares but that's na - t'ral. ___

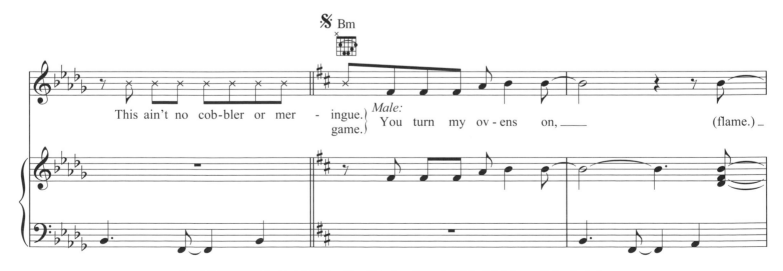

This ain't no cob-bler or mer - ingue.}
game.} *Male:* You turn my ov-ens on, ___ (flame.) ___

ISN'T THIS THE WORLD

Words and Music by PHARRELL WILLIAMS,
CHAD HUGO and JOHN WILLIAMS

Moderate Soul

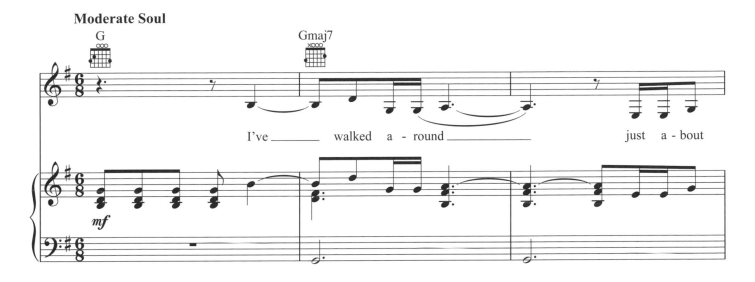

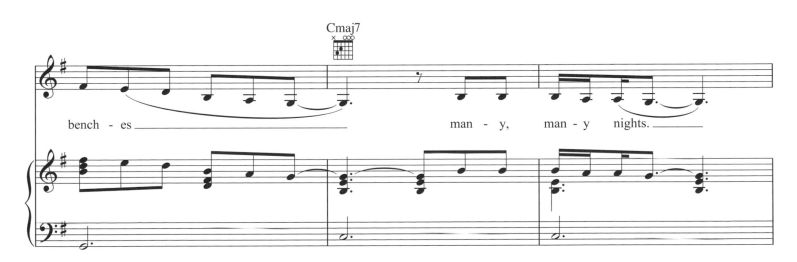

CRYSTAL CLEAR

Words and Music by
PHARRELL WILLIAMS

Moderate Soul

Look what you've done to me. __

You made me be - have like I would - n't ev - er. I know you're the

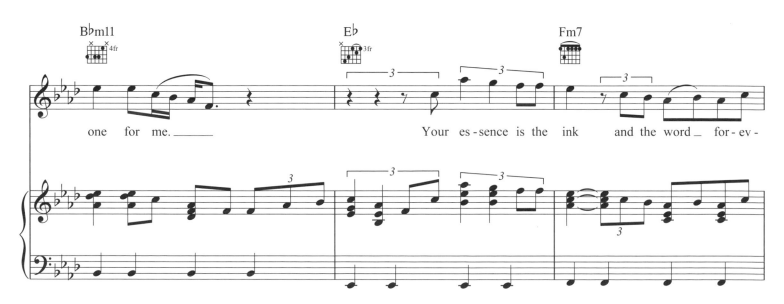

one for me. _____ Your es - sence is the ink and the word __ for - ev-

JALAPEÑO

Words and Music by
PHARRELL WILLIAMS

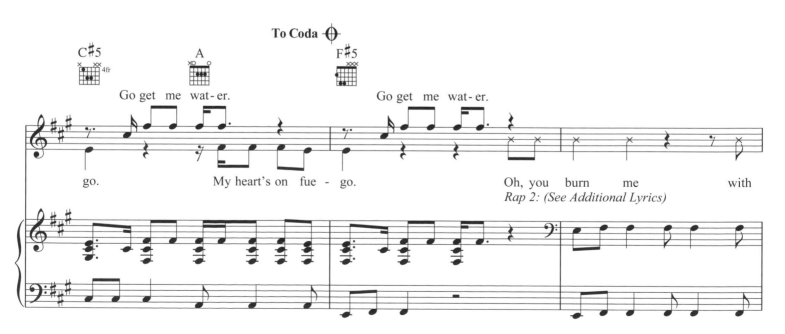

I'm hot! ____ Woo! _ I'm hot! ____ Woo! _ I'm hot! _

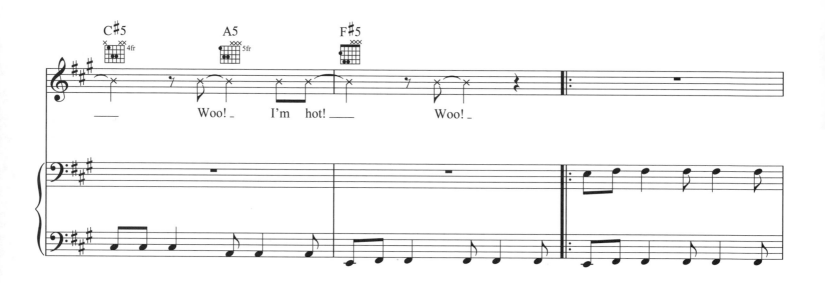

____ Woo! _ I'm hot! ____ Woo! _

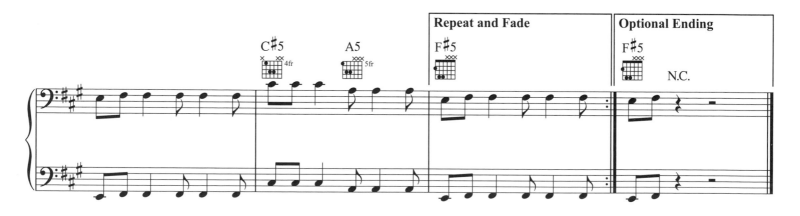

Repeat and Fade

Optional Ending

Additional Lyrics

Rap 2: Hot dang
You burn my kiss off
Coming out the water
Like a Soviet missile

How's it only better
How to say forever
Sure to raise my pressure
Take me out on a stretcher

I SEE A VICTORY

Words and Music by PHARRELL WILLIAMS
and KIRK FRANKLIN

(is with me). — Oh, let them laugh a - bout_ it; don't
So_ I_ tal - lied all my loss - es and I

wor - ry what the doubt-ers say - ing. Yes, it's an up-hill bat - tle, but
turned_ them_ in - to les - sons. And what seemed_ to be less,___ I

To Coda ⊕

guess who else is play - ing. The next time y'all in ac - tion and the
turned them in - to bless - ings. See, I'm not try - ing to lose_ you, but the

ghost is in the room, _ watch it work through the mass - es, you